LET'S PLAY! LITTLE CHAMPS

GYMNASTICS

RYAN JAMES

NorwoodHouse Press

Library of Congress Cataloging-in-Publication Data

Names: James, Ryan.
Title: Gymnastics / Ryan James.
Description: Buffalo, NY : Norwood House Press, 2025. | Series: Let's play! little champs | Includes glossary and index.
Identifiers: ISBN 9781684502387 (pbk.) | ISBN 9781684502394 (library bound) | ISBN 9781684502400 (ebook)
Subjects: LCSH: Gymnastics--Juvenile literature.
Classification: LCC GV461.3J359 2025 | DDC 796.44--dc23

Published in 2025 by
Norwood House Press
2544 Clinton Street
Buffalo, NY 14224

Designer: Ocean Books
Editor: Kim Thompson

Photo credits: Cover, pp. 1, 7, 13, 15Master1305/Shutterstock.com; pp. 5, 21 SeventyFour/Shutterstock.com; p. 6 Julie Dash/Shutterstock.com; p. 9 Dmytro Vietrov/Shutterstock.com; p. 11 Light and Vision/Shutterstock.com; p. 12 ITALO/Shutterstock.com; p. 17 Svitlana Bezuhlova/Shutterstock.com; p. 18 Michael C. Gray/Shutterstock.com; p. 19 Air Images/Shutterstock.com

Printed in the United States of America

CPSIA compliance information: Batch #CW25NHP: For further information contact Norwood House Press at 1-800-237-9932.

TABLE OF CONTENTS

What Is Gymnastics?

Gymnastics is a fun sport. Gymnasts use strength and **flexibility** to jump, spin, and balance. Gymnastics teams compete at **meets**.

The Uniform

Tight-fitting, stretchy leotards or **singlets** let gymnasts move easily.

Some gymnasts wear comfortable shorts, T-shirts, or pants.

Gymnasts do not want to slip and fall. Some wear special slippers with extra grip. Others go **barefoot** so they can feel the floor better.

The Events

At a meet, gymnasts compete in different events. They use special equipment, or **apparatus**, for each event.

For the vault event, gymnasts run and jump onto a springboard. They flip over a vaulting table and land on their feet.

For the balance beam event, gymnasts walk, jump, and flip on a long, narrow beam.

For the floor exercise event, gymnasts do flips and dance moves on a big mat.

For the uneven bars event, gymnasts do **tricks** in the air. They swing and flip between two bars at different heights.

Boys have different events than girls. For the **pommel horse** event, they hold handles as they swing their legs. For the still rings event, they hold rings while doing tricks in the air.

The Moves

Gymnasts learn lots of moves and tricks. For front and back handsprings, gymnasts push off the floor with their hands before flipping.

For backbends, gymnasts bend backward to touch the floor.

For front and back walkovers, gymnasts bend backward or forward and flip their legs over their head.

For a split leap, gymnasts jump high and spread their legs wide in the air.

How to Be Meet-Ready

Gymnasts should eat healthy foods like fruits, vegetables, and lean meats. They should drink plenty of water. Getting enough sleep gives them **energy** to perform at their best.

GLOSSARY

apparatus (ap-uh-RAT-uhs): equipment used for performing sports, especially gymnastics

barefoot (BAIR-fut): without socks or shoes

energy (EN-ur-jee): the ability to do work

flexibility (FLEK-suh-bil-i-tee): the ability to bend easily

meets (meets): sports competitions between teams

pommel horse (PUHM-uhl hors): a padded piece of gymnastics apparatus that sits on the floor, that has two handles, or pommels, on top, and that is used for balancing, rotating, and swinging moves

singlets (SING-glits): sleeveless leotards with built-in shorts

tricks (triks): amazingly skillful actions

THINKING QUESTIONS

1. What do gymnasts wear?
2. Why do some gymnasts wear special slippers?
3. Why do you think the balance beam might be difficult to perform on?
4. Why do gymnasts need to eat healthy foods?
5. What qualities do you think a good gymnast has?

INDEX

ABOUT THE AUTHOR

Ryan James lives in the western part of North Carolina with his rescue dog Bailey. As a child, he would search for creepy crawlies as he hiked through the forest near his house. When he's not on the hiking or biking trail, he is cheering on his favorite baseball and football teams.